Understanding
The Realm
of the
Spirit

An Apostolic-Prophetic Teaching on Navigating in the Holy Ghost

Will Thomas

DREAMWISE PUBLISHING

Columbus, GA

A Dreamwise Company

To Minister Kimberly Smith
I pray this book blesses you on your journey!

Blessings!
- Pastor Will

Understanding the Realm of the Spirit

For information contact :
Dreamwise Publishing
PO Box 6144
Columbus, GA 31917
https://www.dreamwisepublishing.com

Cover design by Will Thomas
ISBN: 978-1-7370555-2-5

Limits of Liability and Disclaimer :

The Author and Publisher shall not be liable for misuse of this material. This book is strictly for educational and informational purposes.

Dedications

Hebrews 1:3
Who being the brightness of his glory, and the express image of his person, and upholding all things by the word of his power, when he had by himself purged our sins, sat down on the right hand of the Majesty on high.

Psalms 18:35-36
Thou hast also given me the shield of thy salvation: and thy right hand hath holden me up, and thy gentleness hath made me great. Thou hast enlarged my steps under me, that my feet did not slip.

Jude 1:24-25
Now unto him that is able to keep you from falling, and to present you faultless before the presence of his glory with exceeding joy, To the only wise God our Savior, be glory and majesty, dominion and power, both now and ever. Amen.

Contents

Acknowledgments

Let me start at the beginning—that is the beginning of all things, God. To Him, I owe everything. My life, my breath, and my thoughts originated with Him, belong to Him, and are at His disposal to use. In Him, I live, move, and have my being. This project could have never "manifested" without Him. I pray continually for clean hands and a pure heart.

To my Shepherd, Apostle Christopher Abernathy. Thank you for the apostolic and prophetic vision from God that you have conveyed, taught, and imparted.

Thank you for your guidance, patience, and dedication to the spiritual growth of your spiritual sons and daughters everywhere. You have been more than a pastor, more than a bishop, and more than an overseer to me. You have also been a father. I have watched you pastor with patience, lead with humility, and persevere with integrity. None of your prophecies concerning me or my family has ever fallen to the ground! You also did not just prophesy this book, but you prayed me through it. I encountered your pastorship at a pivotal sink or swim moment in my life. Thank you for the swimming lessons. I appreciate what you have taught me spiritually. Much of what I understand about the Realm of the Spirit came from and was instructed by you. The pastoring and teaching I receive at True Vine Ministries, International is incomparable. Your Five-Fold ministry is boundless. I am so humbled and honored to be one of your many sons on this earth.

To Elder Grant (Mama GG). Thank you for your gift of intercession and all your prayers and encouragement. You have always believed in me. You have always pushed me. You are the definition of a prayer warrior! You have been a tremendous blessing to me and my family. I praise God for you!

To Elder Johnnie Baker. Thank you for being such a great example of a minister standing in the Five-Fold Ministry Office of the Teacher. Thank you for your prayers and your spirit of excellence.

To Pastor Phillip Horace and Minister Shaundra Horace. Thank you for your friendship, loyalty, integrity, and labor of love. We are in covenant together. Thank you for your love and prayers.

To True Vine. Thank you for the encouragement to write and for the prayers of the righteous. You are such a great cadre of leaders—some of God's best. There is no "family" like you. We are going up!

To Minister Sabrina Thorps. Thank you so much for your gift, your vision, and your help every step of the way. Your idea that day changed everything. This book was in my heart, but you were the vessel that God used to bring it into my now. You have been a tremendous blessing to me and Pastor Cheryl. Dreamwise Publishing is a treasure!

To Chris, Raymond, LaSondra, Quad, Shankequa, Jaey, Madisson, and Makenzie. I hope you find something in this book that brings you to know God in a new way. Your love brought me to know family in a new way.

To Carolyn Thomas, Mama. You were my first Bible teacher. What I learned about God, I learned first from you. I pray this book is all you believed it would be.

To my Mother-in-law, Jessie Mae Streeter, my Sister Denise, my brother Johnny, Minister Terrance Hobbs, and Minister Monique Hobbs. Thank you so much for your prayers and hope.

And finally, to my precious wife, Pastor Cheryl Thomas. You are a gift from God! Your love for me is boundless. I am inspired by your ministry, your prayer life, and your giving. Thank you for loving me the way I needed to be loved and sharing a life with me I never thought I would have. I see the love of God every day in your smile. Thank you for believing in me, especially on the days when I did not believe in myself. Thank you for praying for me, fasting for me, walking the floor at night for me, and speaking life over me. I have learned from your patience, acceptance, loving-kindness, hope, contentment, and determination. You are God's number one fan. Your pursuit of Him has always amazed me. You are so in love with God that you spend every day trying to win another soul. I thank God for the books you will write, the music you will make, the souls you will win, and the lives you will touch. I met you when I did not want to live anymore, and you showed me I had not yet begun to live. You took the broken, shattered pieces of my life and held them close to your heart. Even more, than I did, you saw this book and waited for it to manifest. Thank you for being my wife and absolute best friend.

CHAPTER 1

Spiritual Power

A New Beginning, A New Understanding

It is my earnest prayer that as a reader of this that you not only learn what God has called you to but also, the power He has entrusted to you. Jesus explained this in the Parable of the Sower. Found in Matthew 25:14-30, Jesus tells the story of a man who entrusted his employees each with varying amounts of capital before departing on a trip. When he returned, he questioned them to see what they had done with what he gave them. To the employer's disappointment, only two of the three endeavored to gain a return on his investment. Because Jesus commences this parable with the phrase "the Kingdom of Heaven," we have traditionally associated this scripture with eternal judgment and eternal reward. But I challenge you to look a little deeper into this parable to see what else Jesus is saying. Sure, the employer returning home symbolizes our Lord's Second Coming, and the employer's last words to each employee symbolize the judgment all humanity will receive, but again, I challenge you to see more.

In John 1:12, the Apostle John reveals something about what we possess as believers in Jesus Christ our Lord:

> *John 1:12*
> *But as many as received him, to them gave*
> *the power to become the sons of God, even*
> *to them that believe on his name:*

This power John speaks of is called **spiritual authority**. Spiritual authority is granted by Jesus Christ who made us joint-heirs with Him through our redemption on Calvary. We accept membership into the royal, Holy family by believing in the name of Jesus. As we submit to the leadership of the Spirit of God (the Holy Spirit/Holy Ghost), we then become the **sons of God** because the very essence of sonship is not just belonging to God but exhibiting the attributes of God. Therefore, the purpose of spiritual authority is to have access to spiritual power.

> *Ephesians 10:8*
> *For though I should boast somewhat more*
> *of our authority, which the Lord hath*
> *given us for edification, and not for your*
> *destruction, I should not be ashamed:*

The origin of the power is Jesus Christ Himself. When He died for our sins on the cross, He paid the penalty of death for sin. God told Adam that the penalty for sin was death. The Bible reinforces this when it says, *"the wages of sin is death" (Romans 6:23)*. After dying, Jesus resurrects Himself through the power of the Holy Ghost, proving that the power of the Holy Ghost has victory over death and the grave, and it can give life.

The power of the Holy Ghost is the power of the Spirit of God. Because God adopted us as sons, we have access to that power and the authority by our family name (the Holy Name of Jesus) to use that power. Additionally, there is no gender in God's sonship, only in utility. While God DOES grant SPECIFIC roles to males and females for earthy family relationships, marriage, and reproduction, mankind is a species of both males and females, so women are included in God's sonship and as joint-heirs of Christ.

> *Romans 8:6, 14-18*
> *⁶ The Spirit itself beareth witness with our spirit, that we are the children of God:*
> *¹⁴ For as many as are led by the Spirit of God, they are the sons of God.*
> *¹⁵ For ye have not received the spirit of bondage again to fear; but ye have received the Spirit of adoption, whereby we cry, Abba, Father.*
> *¹⁶ The Spirit itself beareth witness with our spirit, that we are the children of God:*
> *¹⁷ And if children, then heirs; heirs of God, and joint-heirs with Christ; if so be that we suffer with him, that we may be also glorified together.*
> *¹⁸ For I reckon that the sufferings of this present time are not worthy to be compared with the glory which shall be revealed in us.*
> *¹⁹ For the earnest expectation of the creature waiteth for the manifestation of the sons of*

God.

1 John 3:1
Behold, what manner of love the Father hath bestowed upon us, that we should be called the sons of God: therefore the world knoweth us not, because it knew him not.

Remember I told you to take a closer look at what Jesus was saying in the parable earlier? Jesus was not just speaking of eternal judgment and eternal rewards. Jesus was also speaking of authority and power. The employer in the parable entrusted his employees with a certain amount of capital and the authority to use it. He expected them, as his employees to be as productive as he would have been with what he put in their hands. Upon his return, he wanted to see if these employees had been productive and multiplied what he originally gave them. In this parable, the employer is Jesus. Jesus knows that the Father has equipped us with spiritual power from Heaven. Being also joint-heirs with Jesus, we are sons of God and therefore, have the authority to use the power of Heaven, the power of the Holy Ghost. However, having this spiritual authority comes with a responsibility to perform as sons of God—meaning we must be productive and multiply.

In Genesis Chapter 1, God instructs the man and woman He created to be productive and multiply:

> *Genesis 1:28*
> *28 And God blessed them, and God said unto them, Be fruitful, and multiply, and replenish the earth, and subdue it: and have dominion over the fish of the sea, and over the fowl of the air, and over every living thing that moveth upon the earth.*

As sons of God, they had the responsibility to perform as sons and do in the earth what God Himself would do. He gave them the power and the authority to use it.

You will learn later in this book that their spiritual power was upon them. What we gained after the Ascension of Christ and Pentecost, is within us. Nevertheless, the expectation of all of God's sons is the same. They all are expected to produce, multiply, subdue, and dominate! To ensure we will perform as sons of God, God has entrusted us with His Spirit—the Holy Spirit or the Holy Ghost. We are not on the earth to just merely exist; God expects us to act as He would and bring Heaven to earth!

Jesus even instructed us to pray this way:

> *Matthew 6:8-10*
> *Our Father which art in heaven, Hallowed*
> *be thy name. Thy kingdom come, Thy will*
> *be done in earth, as it is in heaven.*

Jesus instructs us to address God as "Our Father." It is important to note here that Jesus is instructing us to call God the same thing He does. He is telling us that as joint-heirs we have the same access to the Father that He has. As sons of God, we have no spiritual limitations or boundaries that bar us from the power of God! We can only be prohibited by our lack of faith or if we do not have clean hands or an evil (unholy) heart:

> *Psalms 24:3-4*
> *³ Who shall ascend into the hill of*
> *the Lord? or who shall stand in his holy*
> *place?*
> *⁴ He that hath clean hands, and a pure*
> *heart; who hath not lifted up his soul unto*
> *vanity, nor sworn deceitfully.*

I hope that you relentlessly seek the father for your manifestation as sons. It is the only way you can tap into the full potential of what he destined you to be.

Like it says in Romans, you were *"predestined to be conformed to the image of Christ" (Romans 8:29)*.

This book is designed to help you learn to navigate in the Realm of the Spirit as a son of God, whether you are a new convert or a seasoned leader in the Body of Christ. This book is both an apostolic and prophetic look at the Realm of the Spirit and how God's sons bring the will of God to pass on earth. It is apostolic in that it teaches the order and structure of the Kingdom of God as well as the configuration of the Realm of God. It is prophetic in that it speaks to God's sons strategically about having eyes to see and ears to hear what the Spirit of God is revealing to those in the posture to receive from the Realm of the Spirit.

This book is also a tool for teaching and learning. If we are to learn about God, then we must learn and understand the intricate way He has done and will do things. We must search out the scriptures to identify patterns and paradigm shifts in God. We error when we see ourselves (as sons of God) separate from the Realm of the Spirit, where we were called to command ever since our creation.

This book will elevate your understanding of the sons of God and the Realm of the Spirit far above songs and hymns in the old church. This book will impress upon you the need to pursue God for the revelation of who He is and what His Word says about who we are as His sons, in the Realm of the Spirit.

CHAPTER 2

Spiritual Foundations

The Bible, Sons, and the Spiritual Realm

Villiam Evans in *The Great Doctrines of the Bible,* provides a great explanation of how the Bible was created. He says that the English word "Bible" derives from the Greek words biblos *(Matt. 1:1)* and bibilion *(Luke 4:17)*, meaning "book." Ancient books were often written on the biblus reed, thus producing the Greek name biblos, which came to be applied to the

20

sacred book. *(Mark 12:26; Luke 3:4; 20:42; Acts 1:20; 7:42.)* 2 Timothy 3:16-17 discusses that the Bible is the inspired Word of God. According to William Evans, the word "inspired" literally means "God-breathed." It is composed of two Greek words: *theos meaning God; and pnein meaning to breathe.* The term "given by inspiration" denotes to the believer that both the Old Testament and New Testament are all from the mouth of God:

> ### 2 Timothy 3:16-17
> *16 All scripture is given by inspiration of God, and is profitable for doctrine, for reproof, for correction, for instruction in righteousness:*
> *17 That the man of God may be perfect, thoroughly furnished unto all good works.*

This statement by Paul in his second epistle to Timothy alludes that God breathed His words into His sons, and they manifested these words into what we have today as the Bible. This should not be so hard to believe considering God's track record of how He uses His breath. *Genesis 2:7* says, *"And the Lord God formed man of the dust of the ground and breathed into his*

nostrils the breath of life; and man became a living soul."
The Hebrew phrase for "The breath of life" is Neshamah
chay (Ney-shamah-kai). This is not the same as rûah
(roo'-akh), which is a Hebrew word for breath.
Neshamah means divine inspiration.

With this knowledge, we now have a different
perspective on Adam, the breath of God, and the sons of
God. God divinely spoke into Adam by breathing into
his nostrils what was on the inside of Himself! This is
how Adam was made in God's image. God breathed
Himself into Adam and created everything on the inside
of Adam that He wanted to be done in Eden. As Adam
operated in Eden, he did the work of God because God's
mind, instructions, essence, and likeness were within
him. So, God followed this process with His other sons
and divinely inspired them as well to write His words
by giving them His thoughts!

The Bible is not just one book, but rather a collection
of writings, so named (*scriptures*), compiled into several
books, being written under the divine inspiration of
God, and are the very words of God. This makes the
Bible, the book of books. Three major religions,
Christianity, Judaism (the religion of Jewish people),
and Islam (the religion of Muslims) consider the Bible,

or portions of it as holy. Christians consider the entire volume as holy and the indisputable Word of God. It is our spiritual guidebook, spiritual road map (in these modern times, a GPS), and our resource manual to living a life by the instructions of our God.

As sons, we see the Bible as God's immediate voice of direction. It is the urgent agenda of Heaven that must be carried out. When we study the Bible as sons, we are reading while simultaneously operating in the posture of prayer. The Bible was authored by people who, under the direction of the Holy Ghost, penned history, prophecy, judgments, songs, poetry, revelation, teachings, genealogies, letters, and visions all about and protruding from the very Spirit of God.

It is a timeless document, in that it speaks to generations of the past, present, and future, all at the same time. It is prophetic in that it speaks from eternity into all-time (*2 Peter 1:21*). It is apostolic in that it governs our way of life and presents to us the tenets of the Kingdom of God and the configuration of the Realm of God. Case in point, the Bible is the most important book ever created and that will ever be created. So, with this knowledge, how can sons ever read the Bible the same? The answer is simple, we cannot.

2 Peter 2:1

21 For the prophecy came not in old time by the will of man: but holy men of God spake as they were moved by the Holy Ghost.

READING AND SEEKING AS SONS

We are all called to be sons of God but not all Christians grasp that concept. For some, the idea of being sons of God seems unattainable. The Bible does not say that. The Bible assures us that the knowledge we learn as sons and the power we have as sons is phenomenal.

2 Timothy 3:14-15 But continue thou in the things which thou hast learned and hast been assured of, knowing of whom thou hast learned them; And that from a child thou hast known the holy scriptures, which are able to make thee wise unto salvation through faith which is in Christ Jesus. All scripture is given by inspiration of God, and is profitable for doctrine, for reproof, for correction, for instruction in righteousness:

*Hebrews 4:12-13 For the word of God is
quick, and powerful, and sharper than any
two-edged sword, piercing even to the
dividing asunder of soul and spirit, and of
the joints and marrow, and is a discerner
of the thoughts and intents of the heart.
Neither is there any creature that is not
manifest in his sight: but all things are
naked and opened unto the eyes of him
with whom we have to do.*

Timothy and the author of Hebrews reveal in their discourse about the Holy Scriptures some important facts:

(1) The scriptures can make one wise or provide one with advanced, rare knowledge *(Timothy 3:14).*

(2) It takes faith to activate the wisdom from the scriptures. This combination of faith and wisdom supersedes natural human intelligence.

(3) The Word of God is powerful enough through the knowledge of revelation and the power of declaration to put a line of defense between the spirit and the soul of a believer, thus empowering their spirit to overpower the soul.

(4) The scriptures disclose information about people's thoughts that are, otherwise, inaccessible.

(5) Because nothing is hidden from God, the sons of God have prophetic access to the knowledge of God through what He has said in His word.

For that reason, intense, consistent, and comprehensive study of the Bible is vital.

We must employ the purposeful study of the Word of God. Because the Bible is your guide to the Realm of the Spirit, how you understand it depends upon how well you grasp the Word of God. For example, purposeful study means that I am not engaging in the routine vocation of making sure I give God an hour in the morning. Purposeful study means that I have a goal in mind. First, my posture is one of a seeker. I must humble my heart, my mind, and everything else within me so my spirit will be able to receive what God will pour out.

Sons read the Bible differently. We couple what we read with whatever God will say additionally in prayer. We combine our prayer with fasting so our spirit will be emptied and cleansed from all impurities and the residue of the world. We release any grudges or any unforgiveness. Mature sons know that the spirit of offense impairs your ability to have divine focus. When you are offended you are stuck in the soulish realm and your ability to engage in effectual prayer is repressed. Remember, you have a goal in mind, so you are trying to remove anything and everything you can that may impair your understanding of the scriptures or that may cause you to miss the voice of God while reading His Word.

You also use prayer before reading to adjust your spirit for whatever the Word of God will say when you read it. You are delighting yourself in Him and being careful to offer sincere praise and worship as a sacrifice to the King. You are praying for clean hands and a pure heart. You are praying for the right alignment with the

Father and for His will to become yours. This must happen if God's sons are to bring Heaven—the Realm of God, to earth.

Prayer after Bible study is also laden with thanksgiving and worship, but now you are asking God to enable you as a son to carry out what He showed you in the Word. Sons cause the Kingdom of God to be manifested in the earth realm. We do the will of God in the earth just as Jesus would.

Advanced sons are also preparing themselves through Bible study to go into the Realm of the Spirit and travel to different dimensions:

2 Corinthians 12:1-4
¹ It is not expedient for me doubtless to glory. I will come to visions and revelations of the Lord.
² I knew a man in Christ above fourteen years ago, (whether in the body, I cannot tell; or whether out of the body, I cannot tell: God knoweth;) such an one caught up to the third heaven.
³ And I knew such a man, (whether in the body or out of the body, I cannot tell: God

knoweth;)

*⁴ How that he was caught up into paradise,
and heard unspeakable words, which it is
not lawful for a man to utter.*

Here, the Apostle Paul was talking about traveling to different dimensions in the Realm of the Spirit—navigating in the Realm of the Spirit. A **dimension**, such as a Heavenly dimension is a location in the Realm of the Spirit, accessed by a gateway or **portal** in which spiritual resources can be obtained for earthly use. A great example of this is found in *Genesis 28:10–19,* where God and His angels appear to the patriarch Jacob in a dream. In the dream, Jacob sees what Christians have called a ladder but was more so a terraced steppe with angels descending and ascending. On top of this terraced steppe was God Himself.

Any place where God or supernatural beings can enter the earth's atmosphere is a portal. The portal leads to a place in the Realm of the Spirit where one who is navigating can access things. As Jacob saw God and His angels, God was confirming to Jacob that he no longer had to scheme to provide for what he needed, being in covenant with God would now be his source.

Sometimes these portals also lead to ungodly dimensions such as Hell. Therefore, Jesus gave us the power to bind and loose—to lock and unlock. Part of navigating in the Realm of the Spirit is using your authority as sons to police spiritual traffic and prevent the gates of Hell from prevailing. For example, through prayer and declaration, we bind sickness so it will not infiltrate and destroy the health of our loved ones.

Sons use the knowledge we have learned from scriptures to pray the prayer of faith *(James 5:15)*. Sons also utilize the authority Jesus gave us as sons to lay hands on the sick so that they can be healed *(Mark 16:18)*. Sons with prophetic and apostolic gifts can see into the Realm of the Spirit. They can see the origin of that sickness and even reveal if it is a generational curse on the bloodline, or a formed weapon to delay the success of the people of God. Intercessors and apostles can pray in the Realm of the Spirit and access a portal to the dimension where generational healing is located to break the vicious cycle the enemy has used to plague an entire family over two generations!

Proverbs 18:21 says, *"Death and life are in the power of the tongue: and they that love it shall eat the fruit thereof."* When some Christians read this scripture, they are reminded about the imperativeness of what comes out of their mouth. When those of us who have come into Godly knowledge as sons read this scripture, we understand it is as clear instructions to decree and declare, to bind and to loose, and to curse or command life. As sons, we are looking to manifest! We search the Word of God, looking for how we can do the will of God on the earth.

> *Romans 15:4 For whatsoever things were written aforetime were written for our learning, that we through patience and comfort of the scriptures might have hope.*

THE BIBLE EXPLAINS ITSELF

The sons of God understand that when you search the Bible, it equips you with ammunition to defeat the enemy. It is a sourcebook of proven strategies for sons of God to utilize in their assault against the enemy. It is a constant source of encouragement to edify the sons of God so they will always have the assurance that they will victoriously prevail against the gates of hell.

The Bible reminds us that we have the authority as the sons of God to operate as Christ would in the earth.

Because we have come into the knowledge that we are sons of God and that there are expectations of performance on us, we must read the Bible differently from a novice new convert. I am sure you have noticed that when a nonbeliever attends a church service or perhaps is invited to Bible Study by a friend, several questions may begin to arise about the imperativeness of the Bible: "Is the Bible really important?" "Do we need to read a book to navigate through life?" "Why can't I just figure this out on my own?" "How can the Bible help me or benefit me?" "Do I need to read the Bible every day of my life, or is it a "one and done" like other books?" As Christians walking into the manifestation of sons of God and successfully navigating in the Realm of the Spirit, we already have these answers! We know that the answers to these and other questions about the importance of the Bible because the Bible speaks loudly and clearly for itself:

Psalm 19:7-11 The law of the LORD is perfect, converting the soul: the testimony of the LORD is sure, making wise the simple. The statutes of the LORD are right, rejoicing the heart: the commandment of the LORD is pure, enlightening the eyes. The fear of the LORD is clean, enduring forever: the judgments of the LORD are true and righteous altogether. More to be desired are they than gold, yea, than much fine gold: sweeter also than honey and the honeycomb. Moreover, by them is thy servant warned: and in the keeping of them there is great reward.

***Luke 24:44** And he said unto them, These are the words which I spake unto you, while I was yet with you, that all things must be fulfilled, which were written in the law of Moses, and in the prophets, and in the psalms, concerning me.*

***John 20:30-31** And many other signs truly did Jesus in the presence of his disciples, which are not written in this book: But these are written, that ye might believe that Jesus is the Christ, the Son of God; believing ye might have life through and* *that his name.*

John 5:39 Search the scriptures: for in them ye think ye have eternal life: and they are they which testify of me.

Matthew 24:35 Heaven and earth shall pass away, but my words shall not pass away.

John 1:1 In the beginning was the Word, and the Word was with God, and the Word was God.

John 1:14 And the Word was made flesh, and dwelt among us, (and we beheld his glory, the glory as of the only begotten of the Father,) full of grace and truth.

John 17:17 Sanctify them through thy truth: thy word is truth.

James 1:22 But be ye doers of the word, and not hearers only, deceiving your own selves.

I Peter 2:2 As newborn babes, desire the sincere milk of the word, that ye may grow thereby:

These scriptures establish some foundational truths about the Word of God and the privileges it extends to us. God's Word is sweet in that it is comforting. It also is comprehensive in that it gives so many examples of how God has extended the invitation to men and women to be His sons. The Word of God is also promising in that it assures us that God will do everything He said He will do. God the Father separates Himself from other deities by way of the scriptures. Our God, the God of Heaven and earth is the only God that guarantees His Word.

CHAPTER 3

Sonship and Revelations

Sonship and Knowledge in the Spiritual Realm

The Bible dispenses powerful knowledge to the sons of God. Do not underestimate the weight of this statement. When the Word of God is consumed by sons of God, we equip ourselves to navigate in the Realm of the Spirit. For a discourse on this, we will hear from one of God's most profound sons, the Apostle Paul. Paul adamantly argued his case for the imperativeness of the knowledge released from the scriptures in the lives of the congregation meeting at Ephesus, which is modern-day Turkey.

Ephesians 3

1 For this cause I Paul, the prisoner of Jesus Christ for you Gentiles,

2 If ye have heard of the dispensation of the grace of God which is given me to you-ward:

*3 How that by **revelation** he made known unto me the mystery; (as I wrote afore in few words,*

4 Whereby, when ye read, ye may understand my knowledge in the mystery of Christ)

*5 Which in other ages was not made known unto the sons of men, as it is now **revealed** unto his holy apostles and prophets by the Spirit;*

6 That the Gentiles should be fellowheirs, and of the same body, and partakers of his promise in Christ by the gospel:

7 Whereof I was made a minister, according to the gift of the grace of God given unto me by the effectual working of his power.

8 Unto me, who am less than the least of all saints, is this grace given, that I should preach among the Gentiles the unsearchable riches of Christ;

⁹ And to make all men see what is the fellowship of the mystery, which from the beginning of the world hath been hid in God, who created all things by Jesus Christ:

¹⁰ To the intent that now unto the principalities and powers in heavenly places might be known by the church the manifold wisdom of God,

¹¹ According to the eternal purpose which he purposed in Christ Jesus our Lord:

¹² In whom we have boldness and access with confidence by the faith of him.

¹³ Wherefore I desire that ye faint not at my tribulations for you, which is your glory.

¹⁴ For this cause I bow my knees unto the Father of our Lord Jesus Christ,

¹⁵ Of whom the whole family in heaven and earth is named,

¹⁶ That he would grant you, according to the riches of his glory, to be strengthened with might by his Spirit in the inner man;

¹⁷ That Christ may dwell in your hearts by faith; that ye, being rooted and grounded in love,

¹⁸ May be able to comprehend with all saints what is the breadth, and length, and depth, and height;

¹⁹ And to know the love of Christ, which passeth

knowledge, that ye might be filled with all the fulness of God.

20 Now unto him that is able to do exceeding abundantly above all that we ask or think, according to the power that worketh in us,

21 Unto him be glory in the church by Christ Jesus throughout all ages, world without end. Amen.

Paul introduces some excellent points in this passage of scripture. He first tells the Ephesians that there is a dispensation of grace released by God that will cause Gentiles (non-Jewish believers) to now have access to the same promises God originally bestowed upon the House of Israel. This means of sonship that Paul refers to as fellowheirs are not just for those who are genetically Jewish but for whoever believes in the name of Jesus and manifests the works of Christ.

Then there is the concept of revelation. **Revelation** is divine understanding or knowledge given to us by God concerning Himself, or what He has done, is doing, and will do (Eph 1:17). When we read the Bible, God prepares our hearts that we might receive a revelation of Christ (who He is and what that means for us) who changes our minds from a carnal focus onto a spiritual focus. Paul says that God, through revelation, got him to understand something extremely complicated and difficult to comprehend. The revelation that Paul received benefits the Church at Ephesus, as well as Christians today, greatly because Paul is now able to teach them the mysteries of God. The mysteries which they, not being Jewish and unfamiliar with the culture and religion of the Jews, may have found themselves struggling to understand. So instead of trying to understand God, they must understand Paul who explains God to them.

As for sons, revelation is an urgent tool:

2 Corinthians 2:14
Now thanks be unto God, which always causeth us to triumph in Christ, and maketh manifest the savour of his knowledge by us in every place.

According to Paul, God not only causes us to triumph as sons of God using the authority of Christ's name, but God also releases revelation to us which here is depicted as the aroma of knowledge. It is not just mere information, but this knowledge has the power, just like a strong smell, to change the atmosphere. Revelation is not just hearing the Word of God. Revelation is the disclosing of new perspectives about the Word of God, about God Himself, the Realm of the Spirit, or even past, present, and future events on earth:

Deuteronomy 29:29

The secret things belong unto the Lord our God: but those things which are revealed belong unto us and to our children forever, that we may do all the words of this law.

Luke 24:31-33

32 And they said one to another, Did not our heart burn within us, while he talked with us by the way, and while he opened to us the scriptures?

Matthew 11:25

At that time Jesus answered and said, I thank thee, O Father, Lord of heaven and earth, because thou hast hid these things from the wise and prudent, and hast revealed them unto babes.

Matthew 16:17

And Jesus answered and said unto him, Blessed art thou,

*Simon Barjona: for flesh and blood hath not **revealed** it unto thee, but my Father which is in heaven.*

As Paul explains to the Church at Ephesus, because of revelation, they are now able to enter sonship with God. Paul even addresses them as "fellow heirs" to emphasize how they now reign with Christ as He and them collectively reign with God the Father in the Kingdom. Paul throws in a teaspoon of humility by confessing that he is no better than any of the Ephesians, but he is made a minister by the grace of God. That same grace connected him to them so that they may get this new revelation of who God is and who they are in Christ.

Perhaps the most impactful part of Ephesians 3 is verses 9-11 which says:

⁹ And to make all men see what is the fellowship of the mystery, which from the beginning of the world hath been hid in God, who created all things by Jesus Christ:
¹⁰ To the intent that now unto the principalities and powers in heavenly places might be known by the church the manifold wisdom of God,
¹¹ According to the eternal purpose which he purposed in Christ Jesus our Lord:

Paul is proclaiming that the purpose of his preaching to the Gentiles is so that ALL mankind can come to understand the message of the Bible, which had not yet been printed. The message that we are divinely and genetically connected to God the Father by Jesus Christ (as sons), and those things which were not revealed even to the angels will be revealed to us, in us, and by us, through the power of God's Spirit working in us.

He further encourages the Ephesians to find their strength in Christ and endure all of life's challenges through being filled with the same love Christ operated in while He was here on earth. He concludes this awesome dissertation by assuring the Church at Ephesus that there is no force anywhere more powerful than that of our God. Because He can do anything, He is worthy of all glory.

So, our conclusion to this matter is that we need the Bible to understand our sonship—that is, who we are in relation to who God is. In Him, we live, we move, and we have our being, but without the Word of God confirming that proclamation, we may never come into that realization. Consider the fact that without the Bible, you may never come into the knowledge of your purpose on earth as sons. You may never know, outside of reading the Word of God, why you are here.

Would you want to take the chance of living your life by happenstance and never making calculated moves towards the progression of a goal in your life? Are you ok with not having a connection with a stronger force, a guiding hand, and saving power? Are you willing to die and depart from this life, as we know it, without ever knowing if you accomplished what you were supposed to accomplish while you were here? Through the study of the Bible and revelation from the Realm of the Spirit, we come into the knowledge of who God has called us to be as sons; not just collectively, but individually!

CHAPTER 4

All Realms Are Not Spiritual

The Realm of the Spirit and The Realm of the Flesh

We learned in the Gospel of John Chapter 3 from Nicodemus and his conversation with Jesus that you have to be born again or born of the Spirit, to understand the things of the Spirit. When we say "spirit" of course we are referring to the Holy Spirit, or

Holy Ghost, the third part of the Holy Trinity. The Bible says there are three that bear record or witness in Heaven the manifestation of the works of God (1John 5:7). That is God the Father, God the Son (called Jesus the Christ or Messiah), and the Holy Ghost. So please understand that the Holy Spirit nor the Realm of the Spirit is logical. One may attempt to defend it by the measures of reason in a logical argument but belief and operation in the spirit and the Realm of the Spirit is a matter of faith.

The carnal or the natural mind cannot understand God, the Holy Spirit, or the Realm of the Spirit for that matter. The Bible tells us in *Romans 8:7* that the carnal or natural mind is enmity against God or in other words, the mind of the flesh is hostile to God. Furthermore, the NIV Bible builds an even stronger case in their translation when it says in verse 8 that *"those who are in the realm of the flesh cannot please God."* So, let us take this opportunity to formally introduce two realms: The realm of the flesh and the Realm of the Spirit. The real problem comes when we fail to realize the existence of both and fail to tap into the latter.

To understand the Realm of the Spirit, the Bible warns us that our natural mind will not do us any good.

The Bible says in *Romans 8:6, "For to be carnally minded is death; but to be spiritually minded is life and peace."* Well, what kind of mind do we need to have to access the Realm of the Spirit? *Philippians 2:5 says, "Let this mind be in you, which was also in Christ Jesus".*

Paul exclaims to us in his letter to the Romans in the 7th chapter and the 18th verse, *"For I know that in me (that is, in my flesh,) dwelleth no good thing."* The enemy knows this and therefore tries to keep us in the realm of the flesh so we will not access the Realm of the Spirit. That is the essence of the enemy's strategy against you. He knows that *2 Corinthians 10:3-4* says, *"For though we walk in the flesh, we do not war after the flesh: (For the weapons of our warfare are not carnal, but mighty through God to the pulling down of strongholds;)."*

You are not strong in your flesh. I do not care how many weights you lift or how many miles you can run. There is nothing in your flesh that can conquer the devil. But when you access the Realm of the Spirit, you find all the weapons you need to combat the devil. So, the enemy blocks you from the Realm of the Spirit by occupying you with fleshly things and causes you to fight fleshly battles.

For example, the enemy seeks to occupy your flesh

with sickness. He sends diseases your way. The people of God who have less understanding of the devices of the enemy respond in their flesh. They start going on the internet to Google the symptoms without praying first or reading scriptures on healing. They start calling family members to reach out for support. And when they finally seek the Lord in prayer, it is a plea of help and a cry from a place of fear and defeat. They fail to stand on anything God has said! This is the fleshly response. Soon they will take on even more symptoms and a more mature form of the disease. Why?

Jesus said in *Mark 3:27, "No man can enter into a strong man's house, and spoil his goods, except he will first bind the strong man, and then he will spoil his house."* Jesus told Peter in *Matthew 16:19, "And I will give unto thee the keys of the kingdom of heaven: and whatsoever thou shalt bind on earth shall be bound in heaven: and whatsoever thou shalt loose on earth shall be loosed in heaven."*

The realm of the flesh consists of our wants and desires. It seeks to fulfill a need but not necessarily fulfill the will of God. When Satan came to tempt Jesus in Matthew Chapter 4, he appealed to the flesh of Jesus. To get the advantage over Jesus he suggests that Jesus satisfy His flesh:

> *¹ Then was Jesus led up of the Spirit into*
> *the wilderness to be tempted of the devil.*
> *² And when he had fasted forty days and*
> *forty nights, he was afterward an*
> *hungered.*
> *³ And when the tempter came to him, he*
> *said, If thou be the Son of God, command*
> *that these stones be made bread.*
> *⁴ But he answered and said, It is written,*
> *Man shall not live by bread alone, but by*
> *every word that proceedeth out of the*
> *mouth of God.*

Jesus quickly recognized this as an attack of the enemy and affirmed that as the Son of God, His existence is sustained by the Word of God! Jesus did not allow His flesh to lord over His spirit but, He used the Word of God to invigorate His spirit man so it would command the flesh instead.

A similar situation happens in the Book of Daniel. In chapter 1, Daniel and three other Judah tribesmen were selected by the Babylonians to work for King

Nebuchadnezzar, but not until they first completed a training program that lasted three years. While this may seem like a promotion or career move to some, it was a plot of the enemy to turn some of God's best sons into idol worshippers. Daniel, Hananiah, Mishael, and Azariah were given a command by the prince of the eunuchs, those in charge of such young men, to eat the daily portion of food and wine supplied to them. Daniel in the company refused to do so. Daniel led this protest because he understood the implications of following the ritual diet of idol worshippers. Daniel, instead, proposed to the prince of the eunuchs to allow him and the other Tribe of Judah tribesmen to eat vegetables and drink water and then come back to observe their appearance and performance. Daniel and the other young men resisted the desire of the flesh in both what they were to eat as well as not giving in to peer pressure. Because of Daniel's decision, God blessed him and the other young men of Judah. As a result, their performance as sons of God far exceeded the performance of the sons of men.

Daniel, as a son of God, went into the Realm of the Spirit and put a demand on the hand of God to touch his and the other young men's bodies. We do not know the actual words he might have prayed, but we do know that he successfully navigated in the Realm of the Spirit. Not only did Daniel and the other guys look better, but they also performed better in both natural and spiritual abilities.

If you do not access the Realm of the Spirit, you will not bind anything, you will not defeat anything. When the enemy tries to bring the fight to you, your job is to immediately access the Realm of the Spirit. Begin to pray in the Realm of the Spirit using your prayer language of Tongues. Start speaking every scripture you know that you can find which addresses the attack Satan is bringing. Declare the Word of God over your life. Grab your weapons and enter the Realm of the Spirit!

As you enter the Realm of the Spirit, start declaring *Isaiah 54:17, "No weapon that is formed against thee shall prosper!"*

Declare *Exodus 23:25, "And ye shall serve the Lord your God, and he shall bless thy bread, and thy water; and I will take sickness away from the midst of thee."*

Declare *Isaiah 53:5, "But he [was] wounded for our transgressions, [he was] bruised for our iniquities: the chastisement of our peace [was] upon him; and with his stripes we are healed."*

Declare *Deuteronomy 7:15, "And the LORD will take away from thee all sickness..."*

As sons of God, we especially must learn to bind sickness and loose healing. It must be second nature. Satan wants to keep you sick because he knows once you experience a miracle, you will understand that you can go into the Realm of the Spirit and obtain everything you have gained by way of the cross. The devil knows that if you fail to experience God's manifestation you will lose faith!

The Bible says that the woman with the issue of blood had gone from doctor to doctor but when she heard of Jesus, she threw away the doctor's business cards and started saying, *"If I can but touch his garment I will be made whole" (Matthew 9:19-21 Mark 5:25-34).* Perhaps she had heard *Malachi 4:2* that says, *"But unto you that fear my name shall the Sun of righteousness arise with healing in his wings."* Doesn't *Romans 10:17* say, *"So then faith cometh by hearing, and hearing by the word of God?"* So, when you do not hear and when you do not speak, your faith diminishes! When you lose, faith how can you please God? How can you access the Realm of the Spirit? How can you get what you need? What are you hearing? What are you speaking? Are the words you are speaking in the fleshly realm or the Realm of the Spirit? Are you binding and loosing or just crying and complaining? What is coming out of your mouth?

Remember your performance expectations and that you are a son of God! Sons perform in the earth and the Realm of the Spirit as God would and as Jesus would. When God wants to make more of something, He speaks it into existence. God's reproductive organ is His mouth. Therefore, He put the same power in our tongues as Sons. We have the power to say something, and it appears.

Job 22:28 Thou shalt also decree a thing, and it shall be established unto thee: and the light shall shine upon thy ways.

CHAPTER 5

Spiritual Equipment

*How Sons Are Made Complete in the
Realm of the Spirit*

et's go somewhere now. I want to take you to
Eden. Why Eden? Because Eden is a realm. It was a
spiritual realm on earth. How do we know that?
Because God entered the garden without being called,
summoned, or invoked. Think about the timing here.
This is before the building of the temple, before the

construction of the tabernacle, before the carving of the Ark of the Covenant. This proceeds Mount Sinai and the burning bush.

See, in the present Post Ascension period, we no longer sacrifice goats, bulls, and sheep to invoke the presence of God. In this present age, we invoke the presence of God with our thanksgiving, our praise, and our worship. Jesus was the last blood sacrifice. In the Old Testament, a slaughtered animal had to be placed on an altar and set afire to honor God. Men had to wait on God to show up.

When Moses went up on the mountain to see God, he was there so long the Israelites thought he had died. They thought he was not coming back so they took the gold God had given them from Egypt as a wealth transfer and constructed a golden calf. Well, again, Eden precedes that. Adam made no sacrifices in the garden. Adam did not kill anything. Adam did not burn anything and neither did the woman. Why is that? Because Eden was the garden of God. It was the realm where He placed one of His most prized creations. He made a creature unlike the other animals, fish, birds, and insects. This creature was made in God's image and

God's likeness. He was like God. He had no sin, neither was he born into sin like me and you. He was created from the earth and then placed in the realm of Eden to operate and manage it.

When God wanted Adam to have a counterpart, He did not go outside of the realm of Eden. He created a creature from the other creature that was already like God. The realm of Eden was just as the presence of God is. There was the fullness of joy. It was just like what *Colossians 2:10* says, "*we are complete in him.*" There was nothing that Adam or the woman needed or desired that was not there. There was a river with four parts that watered the garden. One of the rivers encompassed another land that had gold and onyx. Adam never planted anything there. It was there when he got there. His job was to speak over and into what was already there.

I am illustrating something here about the Realm of the Spirit. God has been trying to get you to go into the Realm of the Spirit and access your gifts, potential callings, and assignments. All the resources you need are there. All the healing you will ever need is already there. The promises of God are there waiting for you.

Wealth has already been established there. There is no toil in the Realm of the Spirit. The spouse God creates for us is in the realm.

You may have experienced unnecessary hurt from fake friends because you never accessed the Realm of the Spirit for discernment of the people around you. As sons, God wants us to be complete and lacking nothing. He desires that we call upon his name with confidence as sons and whatever we need while we are on the earth, we can retrieve it from the Realm of the Spirit:

Hebrews 4:16
*Let us therefore come **boldly** unto the throne of grace, that we may obtain mercy, and find grace to help in time of need.*

Amos 3:7, "Surely the Lord God will do nothing, but he revealeth his secret unto his servants the prophets." God wants us to be surrounded by information from the Realm of the Spirit so we can make decisions with ALL the information. 1 Corinthians 14:33 says, "God is not the author of confusion, but of peace, as in all churches of the saints." God is not interested in His sons being inadequate and underequipped. He wants us to have dominion and to subdue. Jesus said in *Luke 10:19*, *"Behold, I give unto you power to tread on serpents and scorpions, and over all the power of the enemy: and nothing shall by any means hurt you."*

Jesus was assuring us that sons of God would never be sent into battle against the enemy without the tools to win and the authority to use them. Jesus even instructed his disciples to wait in Jerusalem after His resurrection until they are given power from the Holy Ghost. He wanted to ensure them that they would have access to the Realm of the Spirit before they launched their ministries. Because we are sons, God makes sure that we have not only the tools and the authority but, also, sound instructions:

> *Isaiah 30:21*
> *And thine ears shall hear a word "behind" thee, saying, This is the way, walk ye in it, when ye turn to the right hand, and when ye turn to the left.*

Access to the Realm of the Spirit means that we have

a connection through the Holy Ghost, allowing us to hear God even during ongoing warfare. Jesus said in *Revelation 2:29 "He that hath an ear, let him hear what the Spirit saith unto the churches."* To hear, you need an established relationship with God built through prayer, study, worship, and declaration that enables you to hear a prophetic word from God in a pivotal time.

The enemy tries to create static for the believer. **Static** is an interfering message or harassment from the enemy that is sent to disturb the sons of God and disrupt communication in the Realm of the Spirit. The enemy always wants to block you from hearing God or prevent you from doing the will of God. For example, in the Garden of Eden, Satan challenged the woman on what God commanded them. He tried to interfere with what they heard God say. Satan released a static, an interfering message that caused the woman and Adam to fall.

The Realm of the Spirit has your weapons. It is your place of ultimate strength. Adam and the woman were indestructible in the realm. They would have lived forever. They would have never gotten sick, and they would have never died. They commanded everything around them.

The enemy understands who he is. Before the fall, he was a cherub that covered the presence of God. He is not and never was a war angel. Michael is the war angel. See, sometimes, you must stay in your lane. Satan knows this and has proof of this. The last time he got in a fight in Heaven, he got hit so hard that Jesus said in *Luke 10:18* "It looked like *"lighting falling from Heaven."* So, the enemy knows that he cannot fight, yet he is a deceiver. He could not defeat Michael the Archangel, but he did manage to deceive other angels. So, he understands his strength.

He knew that Adam and the woman were made like God. He also knew that he did not stand a chance against them in the realm of Eden. If he wanted to defeat them, he would have to deceive them or get them to war against themselves. Adam and the woman were in a place of authority, management, provision, protection, prosperity, and wealth. Satan could not defeat Adam and the woman in the realm of Eden, so he got them to go into the realm of the flesh. He appealed to their sensual nature and asked them to consider that the fruit of the tree was good for food. This is a word for someone. In the flesh, there is only deception because nothing in the flesh is permanent. It is only temporary.

The Bible instructs us in *2 Corinthians 5:16* to *"know no man after the flesh"*. Why? Because you need to know the spirit that controls the person. The Bible says in *1John 4:1, "believe not every spirit, but try the spirits whether they are of God"*. How do I do that? I must access the Realm of the Spirit. I must spend some time on my face praying to God in my heavenly language, fasting, and seeking the wisdom of God. You need to be able to see what God is trying to show you in the Realm of the Spirit!

I want to bring the aspect of danger to the table. The woman got deceived while she was in her realm. She did. Why? The devil tried his signature move. Do you know what he did? He questioned her on the Word of God that had already gone forth. Ok, some of you do not see the danger in that. Well, consider this: How many of you would be able to defeat the devil if he asked you ANY QUESTIONS about the Word of God? While you are pondering on that, I want you to ponder on this: Is your Bible study regime at home strong enough to combat anything the devil confronts you with? Be truthful about this. *Hosea 4:6* says, *"My people are destroyed for lack of knowledge."* Well, guess what the rest of that verse says? It says, *"because thou hast rejected knowledge, I will also reject thee, that thou shalt be no priest to me: seeing thou hast forgotten the law of thy God, I will also forget thy children."* Do you hear that? Are you ready for those kinds of repercussions?

The Realm of the Spirit is eternal, it is not temporal. It is ongoing. The realm of the flesh is temporal. It has an expiration date on it. Things come in and things go out. Things are born and things die. The Realm of the Spirit produces constant things. They are controlled by the Word of God. The only changes come when you allow something out of the Realm of the Spirit to be pulled out by the words that were not meant for you but your lack of knowledge, or your lack of speaking, did not stop it.

Satan got the woman to change her mind about what God had already said. How do you know? Because when God came in the garden, He said in *Genesis 3:11 and 17, "Who told thee that thou wast naked? Hast thou eaten of the tree, whereof I commanded thee that thou shouldest not eat?"* In verse 17 God says, *"Because thou hast hearkened unto the voice of thy wife, and hast eaten of the tree, of which I commanded thee, saying, thou shalt not eat of it."* God was furious because He spoke a word in the spiritual realm of Eden to Adam. It came out of the mouth of God so that made it as permanent as any other word He had spoken into the earth.

Remember, this is God speaking in a spiritual and eternal realm. Those words do not change. They are as permanent as *"let there be light"*. Isn't the sun still here? God spoke things in Eden that would have never changed for the rest of the age of the earth! We would have never died or never been without prosperity! We would still be speaking to the ground, and it would yield food without us physically planting it.

God made Adam like Him. God's reproductive organ is in His mouth. When God wants to make more of something, He speaks it. When he spoke, seed was in His voice! Adam was made like God. He was the manifestation of God in the earth. When he spoke, seed was also in his voice! That is why he was able to name all the animals and give them their characteristics and nature. God had planted directly into Adam.

God's Word to Adam was eternal and should have never been violated. It was supposed to never change. However, Satan got Adam and the woman to hear a different voice other than God while they were inside of the same realm in which they heard it. That is why God said, "because you chose to *hearken*," or hear, "the voice of your wife." Inside of the realm of the spirit, Adam chose another truth over the eternal Word of God! Therefore, Adam's world turned upside down. He was no longer standing on the word of God. When you chose another word over God's word, that is rebellion. Now, who in this scenario would know a little something about rebellion? The devil always leaves his footprint.

Adam lost the image and likeness of God because he no longer agreed with the Word of God. He spit out the seed. Therefore, God asked the woman, "*What is this that thou has done?*" He was asking her does she understand the extent of what has happened here. Of course, Satan fully understood. It was his plan. He came to Jesus the same way. He understood that in the wilderness Jesus was not only in the flesh but, after forty days, He was weak in the flesh.

Jesus had been fasting for 40 days without a constant source of water. Satan asks him not a spiritual question but a question in the realm of the flesh. In Matthew 4:3, Satan says, "If thou be the Son of God, command that these stones be made bread."

It is a reason why you need the Armor in Ephesians

Chapter 6. The Bible says, "Put on the whole Armor of God, that ye may be able to stand against the wiles of the devil." Whole Armor means completely protect yourself. Keep in mind that this is a spiritual process. That means that it takes more than reading a daily devotion. It takes more than "now I lay me down to sleep". It takes dedication to the process of spiritual defense! That word "wiles" means schemes. We learned that the devil only has one scheme and that is he tries to get you to either speak something else other than the Word of God, or he tries to get you to believe something else other than the
Word of God.

Verse 12 says, "For we wrestle not against flesh and blood, but against principalities, against powers, against the rulers of the darkness of this world, against spiritual wickedness in high places." The Apostle Paul is warning you that you are not fighting people. These are ancient spirits of different rank who know what man fall privy to. They are the influences or the "spirits you didn't want to discern" that drive people of all cultures and of all societies to do the evil that they do. They influence laws, they influence mass murders, and they have influenced whole generations. Paul is saying, by the way, this is who you are fighting. Therefore, you have got to access the spiritual realm.

Verse 13 says, "Wherefore take unto you the whole Armor of God, that ye may be able to withstand in the evil day, and having done all, to stand." So, the instructions tell us to do what? Complete your spiritual defense. Fortify yourself on every side in the spirit so you will be prepared for the "evil day." What is the evil day? That is when spiritual and eternal beings that you refused to get prepared for, have plotted to enter the realm of the flesh, enter time, and come against you. That is the evil day. But Paul said, *"having done all, to stand"*. What does that mean? It means that when I suit up in the spirit, even though they were planning this attack, I will be able to stand against it and not be moved! I will not be destroyed! No weapon formed against me shall prosper! My weapons are mighty and strong enough to pull down these strongholds!

Ok, so how do I fortify? Well, in verse 14, it says, "Stand therefore, having your loins girt about with truth, and having on the breastplate of righteousness." Your loins cover your reproductive parts. If you are going to speak the truth over any area of your life it needs to be right there! And this goes several ways.

(1) Speak the truth over what you are and what you are supposed to be anatomically and in the spirit. If you are a man speak the truth about what God says about being a man. If you are a woman then speak scriptures about what God has spoken over the life of women.

(2) Declare the truth about your generation. Not what the devil says. See sometimes we fall into sin but sometimes we are held captive by what the enemy has tried to slip into our bloodline. Jesus said in Matthew 12:43-45, "When the unclean spirit is gone out of a man, he walketh through dry places, seeking rest, and findeth none. 44 Then he saith, I will return into my house from whence I came out; and when he is come, he findeth it empty, swept, and garnished. 45 Then goeth he, and taketh with himself seven other spirits more wicked than himself, and they enter in and dwell there: and the last state of that man is worse than the first."

The word house in that scripture is the Greek word "Oikos". It does not mean structure or shelter. The word Oikos means "family." The unclean spirit is saying I will return unto the family from which I came! Not the building but the family. When Jesus went to the boy with the demon in him in Mark Chapter 9, Jesus did not cast the devil out right away. Instead, He went to the father and asked, *"how long has he been like this?"* Why would it matter? Jesus has all authority. But in this instance, Jesus was trying to teach his disciples something. He was trying to show them why they needed to learn how to access the Realm of the Spirit for themselves. He saw some differences in this unclean spirit. He asked the father because he was the head of the house. So, Jesus asked the head of the house or the family, "How long has this demon been in your family?"

Sometimes, the enemy goes after the family. Sometimes, he goes after the child before birth. He went after Moses as a child. He tried to kill all the males of Moses' time. When Jesus was born, he influenced Herod to kill every boy under 2 years old in Bethlehem. It is important that as sons of God, we understand that our navigation in the Realm of the Spirit affects more than today, but it also affects tomorrow.

EPILOGUE

When He Appears, We Shall Be Like Him

I hope this book changes how we take our job as sons of God. All of us should take our role of establishing the will of God in the earth as the priority of our life. In Daniel Chapter 10, Daniel had set himself aside to seek the Lord concerning the future. When his answer was delayed, an angel came and alerted him that God did hear Daniel the first day he prayed. However, Daniel's answer had been delayed because the angel with his answer had been in warfare on his way back to Daniel.

Daniel 10:12-13

[12] Then said he unto me, Fear not, Daniel: for from the first day that thou didst set thine heart to understand, and to chasten thyself before thy God, thy words were heard, and I am come for thy words.

[13] But the prince of the kingdom of Persia withstood me one and twenty days: but, lo, Michael, one of the chief princes, came to help me; and I remained there with the kings of Persia.

While we have for years in the church celebrated the fact that an angel visited Daniel, there is a greater occurrence in this lesson. Daniel's prayer was not interrupted by demonic forces. Daniel understood enough about navigating in the Realm of the Spirit as a son of God that he knew how to elevate to a higher dimension in the Realm of the Spirit! This resulted in the prayer being unhindered because Daniel prayed in a dimension higher than where the angels and the demonic opposition was.

Navigating in the Realm of the Spirit should result in answered prayers, diseases irradicated, generational curses dismantled, wealth transferred, the song of the Lord sang, and spiritual growth in our lives. We should be more like Christ than we have ever been in our lives. After all, that is the goal, that when Jesus appears, we as sons of God shall look like the Son of God.

1 John 3:2

*Beloved, now are we the sons of God, and it doth not yet appear what we shall be: but we know that, when he shall appear, **we shall be like him**; for we shall see him as he is.*

While eating some potato chips, I realized that I fed myself differently to write this book. (I am talking about spiritual food of course). I wanted to make sure that I stayed true to how I normally seek God to ensure the best results, but I also knew in my spirit that I desired to do something extra. It was not just about the words I used but more so about the intent of the book. I wanted to say what God wanted me to say. Instead of putting forth my dream work, I wrote in the moment. I fasted every day and then began to write. The skeleton was already in my head and written in fragments, but the re-write was the product of late nights and early mornings with the Lord. I thought I was waiting on Him, but He was waiting until I could hear Him.

As I begin to get to the end of this work, I began to see that God had been writing this book inside of me for a while. God started this when I was a child, sitting in the house reading my mother's Sunday School curriculum and Bible books. I was restricted in my activity outdoors because of asthma and bronchitis but found freedom indoors with Matthew Henry's Commentary and the Broadman's Notes. God advised me not to write all that I know in this book. He assured me that this was the first book but not the only one. So, I worshipped, prayed, and listened for what God would say to me out of the Realm of the Spirit.

In the twilight hours, I found solace in watching my wife sleep and walking around the bedroom speaking to the Lord. The expanse of the night passed quickly and before I knew it, 1 am quickly became 4 am, and then 6 am. So, it was during a slumbering house that I changed.

I had already been published in academia writing history articles and book chapters, and years ago as a reporter for my high school newspaper as well as my college newspaper. Later, I was even published professionally as a freelance writer, but it was this project that mattered the most. Now, I have finally done the work that I know God created me to do. I have written a Christian book. I hope this book is used in Bible studies in various churches and as a tool for personal Christian growth. This book does not answer every question about the Realm of the Spirit, but I think it probably created some.

As I began to write this book about *Understanding the Realm of the Spirit,* God began to minister to me about the power of becoming sons of God. This book was written to be accessible to all sons, no matter where they are in their walk with God. It is a book for the church mother and the intercessor. It is a book for the usher and the lead pastor. It is a book for the youth pastor and the daycare leader. Whatever is in this book that you may want to hear more of and in more in-depth, please contact me and let me teach it to your church or small group. The prophet Joel informed us that God plans to pour out His Spirit on men, women, and children and we will see them prophesy and hear about their dreams and visions *(Joel 2:28).* I feel like we are in that time, even if it is just the beginning. I also feel like this book is a part of that outpouring. It would be fantastic if this book becomes a catalyst for stirring or increasing your access to the Realm of the Spirit.

ABOUT THE AUTHOR

Will Thomas, A Son of God

Will Thomas is passionate about seeing the people of God become who God has called them to be. He has served in almost every capacity in the church from music to helps ministry, outreach, college ministry, and leading God's people as a senior pastor. Known affectionally as "Pastor Will," he presently serves proudly as an associate pastor and an armorbearer at True Vine Ministries, International, in Columbus, Georgia under the pastorship of the founder, Apostle Christopher

Abernathy. Pastor Will's wife, Pastor Cheryl, also serves at True Vine Ministries as Youth Pastor.

Pastor Will was an award-winning high school teacher for over sixteen years. He is a professional historian, completing a Ph.D. in history at Auburn University in Auburn, Alabama, where he is a Presidential Graduate Research Fellow.

Understanding the Realm of the Spirit: An Apostolic-Prophetic Teaching on Navigating in the Holy Ghost is Pastor Will's first book. It was written for all who want to learn how we as sons of God can employ the power of the Holy Ghost to accomplish the will of God.

You can learn more about Pastor Will or read more of his biblical teachings on his website, thebibleblog.org.

For copies of this book, please contact Dreamwise Publishing at **www.DreamwisePublishing.com** or Will Thomas at www.thebibleblog.org.

For booking or to contact Pastor Will, send an email to willthomas@thebibleblog.org.

Will Thomas

Made in the USA
Columbia, SC
26 July 2021